NFL

SUPERSTARS

1985

by Hal Lundgren

ⵕ CHILDRENS PRESS ®
CHICAGO

To the Reader

Included in this book are facts about twenty-five National Football League superstars. They are presented in alphabetical order. You may not agree with our choices. You may have a favorite who is not included. However, we still hope you will enjoy reading about these stars and the teams of the National Football League.

Photo Credits

Steve Schwartz—4, 24; Al Messerschmidt—6, 10, 12, 18, 20, 28, 30, 36, 44, 46, 48, 50; John E. Biever—8; George Gojkovich—Cover, 14, 32, 34; Scott Cunningham—16; Al Kooistra—22; Ron Wyatt—26, 52; Ray De Aragon—38; Nancy Hogue—40; Brian Yablonsky—42; © NFL Properties, Inc. 1982, 1983—56, 57, 58, 59, 60, 61, 62

Cover and interior design by Karen A. Yops

Library of Congress Cataloging in Publication Data

Lundgren, Hal.
  NFL superstars, 1985.

  Summary: Brief profiles of twenty-five football "greats" playing on NFL teams in 1985.
  1. Football players—United States—Biography—Juvenile literature. 2. National Football League—History—Juvenile literature.
  [1. Football players. 2. National Football League—History]
  I. Title.
GV939.A1L86 1985   796.332'092'2 [B] [920] 85-17102
ISBN 0-516-04433-8

1 2 3 4 5 6 7 8 9 10 R 94 93 92 91 90 89 88 87 86 85

CONTENTS

MARCUS ALLEN
running back
Los Angeles Raiders

Born March 26, 1960, in San Diego, California
Attended San Diego Lincoln High School and
the University of Southern California.

When the Raiders slumped after winning the
1981 Super Bowl, everyone seemed to know what
they needed to win again—a game-breaking
running back. They drafted Allen Number 1 in
1982. On January 22, 1984, Allen completed his
second pro season by helping the Raiders defeat
Washington, 38-9, in the Super Bowl.

SECRET WEAPON—It's hard to imagine
Marcus Allen as a secret weapon. He won almost
every important national football honor in 1981 as
a University of Southern California senior,
including the Heisman Trophy. Yet, Allen has
turned into a secret weapon. Purely a running
threat in college, Allen is equally dangerous as a
receiver. In his first three NFL seasons, Allen
rushed for 2,879 yards. He also slipped out of the
backfield and caught 170 passes for 1,749 yards.

BOB BAUMHOWER
nose tackle
Miami Dolphins

Born August 4, 1955, in Portsmouth, Virginia
Attended Palm Beach Gardens, Florida, and
Tuscaloosa, Alabama, High Schools and the
University of Alabama.

A new position emerged in pro football in the
1970s. Teams had used four-man defensive lines
for many years. There were two tackles and two
ends in the four-man line. Then came the change
to three-man lines. A single nose tackle would play
in the middle rather than two tackles. The man
who played nose tackle had to be stronger and
quicker than tackles of the past. Baumhower fits
that description. The nose tackle also has to be
more patient. At least two men block him on every
play. He cannot become angry. In the three-man
line, linebackers—not nose tackles—are expected
to stop the ballcarrier.

NO LONGER A NO-NAME—When Miami
first went to the Super Bowl in 1973, and when
the Dolphins went again in 1983 and 1985, they
were called a team without stars. Not anymore.
Baumhower is now an all-pro defensive lineman.

EARL CAMPBELL
running back
New Orleans Saints

Born March 29, 1955, in Tyler, Texas

Attended Tyler High School and the University of Texas.

Earl Campbell was the first player drafted in 1978. Tampa Bay held the first pick. But Houston wanted Campbell so badly that the Oilers traded five draft choices plus one player for Tampa Bay's first choice in the draft. The trade turned out well for the Oilers. Campbell won three league rushing championships in his first three years. The Oilers went to the playoffs each year. Their three-year record, 32-16, was second best in the league for those three years.

MOVING MAN—In 1978, Campbell rushed for more yards (1,450) than any other first-year player in NFL history. His totals after two, three, four, and five seasons were the highest for any two-, three-, four-, or five-year player in NFL history. Campbell is the only player to rush for 200 or more yards four times in one season.

9

TODD CHRISTENSEN
tight end
Los Angeles Raiders

Born August 3, 1956, in Bellefonte,
Pennsylvania
Attended Sheldon High School in Eugene,
Oregon and Brigham Young University.

He's pro football's busiest tight end. Maybe its
best, too. After not catching a pass his first two
years in the NFL (1979-80), Christensen has
caught 172 passes the past two years. A strong
blocker, he also catches any ball that comes close
to him.

ONE THAT GOT AWAY—Most of the
superstars in this book have played for only one
team. Christensen was released by two other
teams before the Raiders signed him. Dallas
drafted Christensen in 1978 and released him one
year later. The New York Giants had him briefly in
1979 before he was dropped and signed by the
Raiders.

MARK CLAYTON
wide receiver
Miami Dolphins

Born April 8, 1961, in Indianapolis, Indiana
Attended Cathedral High School in
Indianapolis and the University of Louisville.

There was a time not long ago when Clayton
couldn't have played pro football. He's 5-feet-9 and
only 172 pounds. When rules changed and
defensive players weren't allowed to bump a
receiver who had gone five yards downfield,
receivers lighter than 190 pounds had a better
chance. One of the new, light receivers was
Clayton. In only his second season, 1984, Clayton
made 73 catches for 1,389 yards and 18
touchdowns.

TWO OF A KIND—Clayton and Mark Duper,
Miami's other starting receiver, team up to be the
league's most feared pass-catching pair. Duper
caught 71 passes while Clayton was catching 73 in
1984. It surprises most fans that Duper, too,
stands only 5-feet-9.

CRIS COLLINSWORTH
wide receiver
Cincinnati Bengals

Born January 27, 1959, in Dayton Ohio
Attended Astronaut High School in Titusville,
Florida and the University of Florida.

His name is spelled "Cris," not "Chris." That's
not the only unusual thing about him.
Collinsworth isn't as fast as most wide receivers.
He's also a bit tall—6-feet-5—to carry only 192
pounds. But when the ball is snapped, he always
seems to find a way to get open and make the
catch.

HAPPY SURPRISE—When the Bengals drafted
Collinsworth in 1981, they chose a faster and—
they thought—better receiver one round earlier.
They were mistaken. Collinsworth won the
starting job. He refuses to give it up. A mark of
excellence for a receiver is 1,000 yards per year.
Collinsworth has made 1,000 or more yards in
three of his four NFL seasons.

15

ERIC DICKERSON
running back
Los Angeles Rams

Born September 2, 1960, in Sealy, Texas
Attended Sealy High School and Southern
Methodist University.

Every few years, an Earl Campbell or a Marcus
Allen bursts into the NFL with a tremendous
reputation and lives up to that reputation.
Dickerson is one of those players. Big (6-foot-3,
218 pounds), strong, and fast, Dickerson ran for
1,808 yards as a rookie in 1983. He led the league
in yards and attempts (390) while placing second in
touchdowns (18). In 1984 he stunned the football
world by rushing for 2,105 yards to break O.J.
Simpson's single-season record.

PLENTY OF REST—Although Eric Dickerson
was a high-school All-American who starred for
four years at Southern Methodist University, he
was never a full-time college player. Fellow All-
American Craig James of the New England
Patriots was in the same graduating class. The two
alternated at tailback in their last three college
seasons.

TONY DORSETT
running back
Dallas Cowboys

Born April 7, 1945, in Rochester, Pennsylvania
Attended Hopewell High in Aliquippa,
Pennsylvania and the University of Pittsburgh.

Nickname: T.D.

Dorsett is a player who came to pro football
with both talent and a strong wish to improve. He
wasn't tough enough or strong enough to play his
best football in his first season, 1977. He wanted
to be the best, so he lifted weights and ran harder
than most players do in the spring and early
summer. Dorsett is still one of the quickest backs
around, but he's now one of the strongest, too.

THE RIGHT INITIALS—Tony Dorsett is called
"T.D." The initials fit. Before Dorsett retires, he
will have scored more touchdowns than any other
Dallas player. Bob Hayes holds the Cowboy record
with 76.

JOHN ELWAY
quarterback
Denver Broncos

Born June 28, 1960, in Port Angeles,
Washington
Attended Granada Hills, California, High
School and Stanford University.

Have you ever had too much expected of you?
John Elway faced that problem in 1983. He came
into pro football described by some people as "the
best college quarterback ever." Imagine that! As an
NFL rookie playing the most difficult position on
the field, he was expected to be super from his
first game. Even though he played well, some
people unfairly said he was a disappointment.

FAST IMPROVEMENT—Elway, who has one
of the best passing arms in football, keeps getting
better. He completed 47.5 percent of his passes in
1983. He completed 56.3 percent in 1984.

DAN FOUTS
quarterback
San Diego Chargers

Born June 10, 1951, in San Francisco, California
Attended San Francisco St. Ignatius Prep
School and the University of Oregon.

Coaches and players on other teams make
private jokes about the Chargers and how that
team only seems to care about playing offense.
Nobody makes jokes about Fouts. He is one of the
most feared passers in pro football. Fouts will pass
from any spot on the field to any other spot on the
field. In moments when most teams will run, the
Chargers will pass. If San Diego had a better
defense, the Chargers would have won a Super
Bowl by now.

LONG RIGHT ARM—Fouts' arm has produced
more passes in one season, more completions in
one season, and more 300-yard games in a career
than any other quarterback.

MARK GASTINEAU
defensive end
New York Jets

Born November 20, 1956, in Ardmore,
Oklahoma

Attended Round Valley High School in
Springerville, Arizona, Eastern Arizona Junior
College, Arizona State University, and East
Central Oklahoma University.

NFL teams are famous for finding players in
colleges that are not known around the country.
Gastineau is one of those players. As a senior at
East Central Oklahoma University, Gastineau was
chosen in the second round of the 1979 draft.
After only two or three years, it was obvious that
Gastineau's talent would make him more famous
around the country than East Central Oklahoma
University.

DANCING HALTED—When Mark Gastineau
would swoop in and "sack" the quarterback for a
loss, the spirited defensive end would dance as you
have seen Indians dance in movies. You won't see
Gastineau dance again. Such dances were made
illegal in 1984.

ROY GREEN
wide receiver
St. Louis Cardinals

Born June 30, 1957, in Magnolia, Arkansas
Attended Magnolia High School and
Henderson State University.

One of the best compliments a football player
can hear is that he "does everything except drive
the team bus." In other words, the player is willing
to do anything if it will help his team win. Roy
Green is one such player. He once returned a
kickoff a league-record 106 yards for a touchdown.
He has handled as many as 16 punt returns in one
season. He has been a surprisingly good defensive
player. But he's best as a receiver. Green caught 78
passes both in 1983 and 1984.

BIG YARDAGE—Green has the distinction of
gaining 1,000 or more yards in two ways. He did it
as a kickoff return man with 1,005 yards in 1979.
He did it twice (1,227 and 1,555) as a receiver in
1983 and 1984.

STEVE LARGENT
receiver
Seattle Seahawks

Born September 28, 1954, in Tulsa, Oklahoma
Attended Oklahoma City Putnam, Oklahoma,
High School and Tulsa University.

Most receivers fit into two groups. They are
either "speed" or "move" receivers. Largent clearly
fits into the "move" group. Defensive backs cannot
keep up with his moves on pass routes. Largent
isn't a fast receiver or a tall one at 5-feet-11. But
any defense that tries to cover him with only one
defender should expect to lose. No one in the
league catches more consistently than Largent.
From 1978 through 1981, Largent caught between
66 and 75 balls per season. He gained more than
1,000 yards each year.

ONE THAT GOT AWAY—No team thought
enough of Largent in the 1976 draft to pick him in
the first three rounds. Houston finally chose him
in Round 4, but later traded him to Seattle.

JAMES LOFTON
receiver
Green Bay Packers

Born July 5, 1956, in Fort Ord, California
Attended Los Angeles Washington High and
Stanford University.

Lofton could be the Number 1 receiver in
football. His moves might not be as good as
teammate John Jefferson's, but Lofton has the
speed to get behind any defensive back. Lofton
also is durable. He plays in Green Bay's cold
climate, but almost never misses a game.

YOU CAN BE SMART AND PLAY
FOOTBALL, TOO—Lofton proves there is a place
for brains on the football field. His grades were
good enough to get into Stanford, and he
graduated in industrial engineering while there.

NEAL LOMAX
quarterback
St. Louis Cardinals

Born February 17, 1959, in Portland, Oregon
Attended Lake Oswego, Oregon, High School
and Portland State University.

If you like improvement, you'll like Neal
Lomax. He has improved his completion
percentage each season. He has thrown more
touchdown passes in each year. He has improved
his quarterback rating each season. It should come
as no surprise that his improvement has advanced
his team, the Cardinals, to contending status.

OVERLOOKED—Lomax is another example of
a good player who was overlooked because he
didn't play football at a famous college. He went to
Portland State, and who would draft a Portland
State quarterback in the first round? No team
would. But the Cardinals were the lucky team that
took him in round 2 of the 1981 draft.

DAN MARINO
quarterback
Miami Dolphins

Born September 15, 1961, in Pittsburgh,
Pennsylvania
Attended Central Catholic High School in
Pittsburgh and the University of Pittsburgh.

Talk about a surprise. Dan Marino was
considered the fourth or fifth best quarterback
among seniors of the 1982 college season. So 26 of
the 28 first-round draft choices had been used
before it was Miami's turn to choose. The
Dolphins went for Marino. It turned out to be a
wise choice. He led them to the Super Bowl in only
his second season. Marino has the rare
combination of a quick, strong arm and confidence.
He also has the advantage of excellent receivers
and blockers.

TRIPLE-HEADER—Marino is one of those rare
athletes drafted by three professional leagues. He
was Miami's first choice in the 1983 NFL draft, as
well as the first pick of Los Angeles in the 1983
USFL draft. He also was chosen by the Kansas
City Royals in Round 4 of the 1979 baseball free-
agent draft.

ART MONK
wide receiver
Washington Redskins

Born December 5, 1957, in White Plains, New York

Attended White Plains High School and Syracuse University.

Art Monk grew up in a community famous for its major computer company. Like that company, Monk gets open and catches passes like a computer. As a rookie in 1980, a year when he should have been learning his position, Monk was giving lessons on how to catch. He pulled in 58 passes that year. If he can avoid injuries, Monk has a chance to be one of the two or three best receivers in pro football history.

THE BIG YEAR—The Redskins didn't get to the Super Bowl in January of 1985, but it wasn't Monk's fault. He smashed the league record with 106 catches. That was 21 more receptions than the Number 2 receiver in his conference. The leader in the NFL's other conference had 89 catches.

JOE MONTANA
quarterback
San Francisco 49ers

Born June 11, 1956, in Monongahela, Pennsylvania
Attended Monongahela Ringgold High and Notre Dame University.

Montana comes from the rich, small-town-Pennsylvaina quarterback tradition that gave Joe Namath, Ron Jaworski, and others to football. Montana could become the best of the Pennsylvanians because he started so young. He was a starter at age 24 and a Super Bowl winner at 25.

HIS GREATEST SEASON—Montana was big enough to be declared a state in 1981. He led a San Francisco team to the Super Bowl when many people picked the 49ers to finish last in their division. He led them to a second Super Bowl victory in January of 1985.

OZZIE NEWSOME
tight end
Cleveland Browns

Born March 15, 1956, in Muscle Shoals, Alabama

Attended Colbert Country High School in Leighton, Alabama and the University of Alabama.

Cleveland has had many good tight ends contribute to its winning traditions. But none of them has compared with Ozzie Newsome. Most Cleveland tight ends who came before him succeeded in catching many short passes. Newsome catches short passes, but he's also considered one of football's best deep receivers. After catching 38 passes as a rookie, Newsome made at least 49 catches in each of his next six pro seasons. He led the American Conference in 1984 with 89 catches, matching his 1983 total.

FAMILY AFFAIR—Football can be an inherited talent. Ozzie Newsome's cousin, Darrin Nelson, is an outstanding back with the Minnesota Vikings.

WALTER PAYTON
running back
Chicago Bears

Born July 25, 1954, in Columbia, Mississippi
Attended Columbia High and Jackson State
University.

Nickname: Sweetness

One of the busiest and best runners in football
history, Payton led all ballcarriers in attempts from
1976 through 1979. His 402 total rushing attempts
and pass catches in 1979 set the NFL record. So did
his 275 rushing yards in a November 20, 1977
game against the Minnesota Vikings. Payton also
led the NFL with 1,852 yards rushing in 1977. On
October 7, 1984, Payton passed Jim Brown's career
rushing record of 12,312 yards. Brown's record
was one that many people thought would never be
broken.

MAKING THE BEST OF IT—Most running
backs make more yards if they play on a winning
team. Payton would not know about that. In his
first nine seasons with Chicago, the Bears had
only three winning years.

GEORGE ROGERS
running back
Washington Redskins

Born December 8, 1958, in Duluth, Georgia
Attended Duluth High School and the
University of South Carolina.

George Rogers is a "franchise" player. His skill
can turn a weak team into a strong one. The
Saints lost 15 of their 16 games in 1980. Rogers
was a senior at South Carolina that year. The
Saints drafted him in 1981. They won four games
and nearly won several others with Rogers
carrying the ball. In his second season, 1982, New
Orleans finished with a 4-5 record. While most
teams pass more than they run, the Saints
preferred to give the ball to Rogers and dare
defenses to stop him.

Rogers was traded to the Washington Redskins
in 1985.

A BLAZING START—In Rogers' first pro
season, 1981, he rushed for 1,674 yards and led the
league. His total was the highest ever by a rookie.

BILLY SIMS
running back
Detroit Lions

Born September 18, 1955, in St. Louis,
Missouri
   Attended Hooks, Texas, High School and the
University of Oklahoma.

Most grown-ups who watch football have their
ideas about who is the best running back in
football. Some say Earl Campbell, who is the
strongest; or Walter Payton, who is the quickest.
Those who vote for Billy Sims aren't far off the
track. Sims could be the best mixture of talent in
football. He is about as strong as Campbell and
about as quick as Payton. He can do more than
run, too. He catches the ball as well as most wide
receivers. Sims is the sort of back who can stay in
the game whether his team plans to run or pass on
the next down.

A CONSISTENT SCORER—Sims made 13
touchdowns in his first pro season, 1980. He came
back the next year and scored 13 more
touchdowns. His 1980 total led the league.

LAWRENCE TAYLOR
linebacker
New York Giants

Born February 4, 1959, in Williamsburg,
Virginia
Attended Williamsburg Lafayette High School
and the University of North Carolina.

The special-effects experts who helped make
the movies "Star Wars" and "E.T." so successful
must have had something to do with building
Lawrence Taylor. He's tougher than Darth Vader
and gets where he's going as surely as a laser
beam. At 6-feet-3 and 237 pounds, he is
considered the complete linebacker. Taylor is larger
than any back he has to tackle and also faster than
some of the small backs he has to chase. The
Giants have one of the most promising young
defenses in the league because of Taylor.

THE BIG CITY'S BIG LINEBACKER—New
York City has been short of football stars since Joe
Namath left in the 1970s. As long as Taylor plays
for the Giants, New York will have at least one
football star.

JOE THEISMANN
quarterback
Washington Redskins

Born September 9, 1949, in New Brunswick,
New Jersey
Attended South River, New Jersey, High
School and Notre Dame University.

Once Theismann warmed up, there was no
stopping him. Theismann was such a good baseball
player that the Minnesota Twins drafted him.
When he chose football, he spent his first three
pro seasons with Toronto of the Canadian League.
When he returned to the United States to play
football for Washington, he gave defenses a new
problem. Theismann threw the ball as well as most
quarterbacks. But he ran better than nearly all of
the men who played his position. Even today,
when Theismann's receivers are covered, his
quickness makes him a threat to run for a first
down.

BACK-TO-BACK WINNERS—When
Theismann led Washington to victory in the 1983
Super Bowl, it marked the first time the winning
quarterback in two straight Super Bowls was from
the same university. Theismann and Joe Montana,
San Francisco's quarterback in the 1982 Super
Bowl, both attended Notre Dame.

RANDY WHITE
defensive tackle
Dallas Cowboys

Born January 15, 1953, in Wilmington, Delaware

Attended Wilmington Thomas McKean High School and the University of Maryland.

Randy White is an example of what an athlete can do if he is born with talent and works hard to use that talent. He is a complete lineman because he plays excellent football against both running and passing plays. When opponents use extra blockers to keep White away from the ball, it means there are fewer blockers to stop the other Cowboys. Most of those blockers guess White's weight at 260 or 270 pounds, not the 250 he actually weighs.

EXPERIMENT FAILED, PLAYER SUCCEEDED—When Randy White first came to the Cowboys in 1975, he was a linebacker in the Dallas defense. He became one of the game's great players only after he was switched back to the defensive line.

SUPER BOWL
HISTORY

I   January 15, 1967—Green Bay (NFL) 35
at Los Angeles   Kansas City (AFL) 10

II   January 14, 1968—Green Bay (NFL) 33
at Miami   Oakland (AFL) 14

III   January 12, 1969—New York (AFL) 16
at Miami   Baltimore (NFL) 7

IV   January 11, 1970—Kansas City (AFL) 23
at New Orleans   Minnesota (NFL) 7

V   January 17, 1971—Baltimore (AFC) 16
at Miami   Dallas (NFC) 13

VI   January 16, 1972—Dallas (NFC) 24
at New Orleans   Miami (AFC) 3

VII   January 14, 1973—Miami (AFC) 14
at Los Angeles   Washington (NFC) 7

VIII   January 13, 1974—Miami (AFC) 24
at Houston   Minnesota (NFC) 7

IX   January 12, 1975—Pittsburgh (AFC) 16
at New Orleans   Minnesota (NFC) 6

X	January 18, 1976—Pittsburgh (AFC) 21
	at Miami Dallas (NFC) 17
XI	January 9, 1977—Oakland (AFC) 32
	at Pasadena Minnesota (NFC) 14
XII	January 15, 1978—Dallas (NFC) 27
	at New Orleans Denver (AFC) 10
XIII	January 21, 1979—Pittsburgh (AFC) 35
	at Miami Dallas (NFC) 31
XIV	January 20, 1980—Pittsburgh (AFC) 31
	at Pasadena Los Angeles (NFC) 19
XV	January 25, 1981—Oakland (AFC) 27
	at New Orleans Philadelphia (NFC) 10
XVI	January 24, 1982—San Francisco (NFC) 26
	at Pontiac Cincinnati (AFC) 21
XVII	January 30, 1983—Washington (NFC) 27
	at Pasadena Miami (AFC) 17
XVIII	January 22, 1984—Los Angeles (AFC) 38
	at Tampa Washington (NFC) 9
XIX	January 20, 1985—San Francisco (NFC) 38
	at Palo Alto Miami (AFC) 16

NATIONAL CONFERENCE

EASTERN DIVISION

Dallas Cowboys, 1960
Super Bowl winner, 1972, 1978*
Super Bowl runner-up, 1971, 1976, 1979
Other championship seasons, 1966 (conference), 1967
(conference), 1968 (division), 1969 (conference), 1973
(conference), 1976 (division), 1979 (division), 1981
(division)
Colors: royal blue, metallic blue, white

New York Giants, 1925
Super Bowls, none
Championship seasons, 1927 (NFL), 1933 (division),
1934 (NFL), 1935 (division), 1938 (NFL), 1939 (division),
1941 (division), 1944 (division), 1946 (division), 1956
(NFL), 1958 (conference), 1959 (conference), 1961
(conference), 1962 (conference), 1963 (conference)
Colors: blue, red, white

*Super Bowl dates are for January following the season. (The
1977 Dallas Cowboys won the 1978 Super Bowl.)

Philadelphia Eagles, 1933
  Super Bowl runner-up, 1981
  Other championship seasons, 1947 (division), 1948 (NFL),
1949 (NFL), 1960 (NFL)
  Colors: green, white, silver

St. Louis Cardinals, 1920 (moved to St. Louis from Chicago,
1960)
  Super Bowls, none
  Championship seasons, 1925 (NFL), 1947 (NFL), 1948
(division), 1974 (division), 1975 (division)
  Colors: cardinal, white, black

Washington Redskins, 1932 (founded as Boston Braves,
became Boston Redskins, 1933, moved to Washington, 1937)
  Super Bowl winner, 1983
  Super Bowl runner-up, 1973, 1984
  Other championship seasons, 1936 (division), 1937
(conference), 1940 (division), 1942 (conference), 1943
(division), 1945 (division), 1972 (conference), 1984 (division)
  Colors: burgundy, gold

CENTRAL DIVISION

Chicago Bears, 1920 (founded as Decatur Staleys, became Chicago Staleys, 1921; Chicago Bears, 1922)
Super Bowls, none
Championship seasons, 1921 (NFL), 1932 (NFL), 1933 (NFL), 1934 (division), 1937 (division), 1940 (NFL), 1941 (NFL), 1942 (division), 1943 (NFL), 1946 (NFL), 1956 (conference), 1963 (NFL), 1984 (division)
Colors: Orange, navy, white

Detroit Lions, 1930 (founded as Portsmouth Spartans, became Detroit Lions, 1934)
Super Bowls, none
Championship seasons, 1935 (NFL), 1952 (NFL), 1953 (NFL), 1954 (conference), 1957 (NFL), 1983 (division)
Colors: blue, silver

Green Bay Packers, 1921
Super Bowl winner, 1967, 1968
Other championship seasons, 1929 (NFL), 1930 (NFL), 1931 (NFL), 1936 (NFL), 1938 (conference), 1939 (NFL), 1944 (NFL), 1960 (conference), 1961 (NFL), 1962 (NFL), 1965 (NFL), 1972 (division)
Colors: green, gold

Minnesota Vikings, 1961
Super Bowl runner-up, 1970, 1974, 1975, 1977
Other championship seasons, 1968 (division), 1970 (division), 1971 (division), 1975 (division), 1977 (division), 1978 (division), 1980 (division)
Colors: purple, white, gold

Tampa Bay Buccaneers, 1976
Super Bowls, none
Championship seasons, 1979 (division), 1981 (division)
Colors: orange, white, red

WESTERN DIVISION

Atlanta Falcons, 1966
  Super Bowls, none
  Championship season, 1980 (division)
  Colors: red, black, white, silver

Los Angeles Rams, 1937 (founded as Cleveland Rams, moved to Los Angeles, 1946)
  Super Bowl runner-up, 1980
  Other championship seasons, 1945 (NFL), 1949 (division), 1950 (division), 1951 (NFL), 1955 (conference), 1967 (division), 1969 (division), 1973 (division), 1974 (division), 1975 (division), 1976 (division), 1977 (division), 1978 (division), 1979 (division)
  Colors: blue, gold, white

New Orleans Saints, 1967
  Super Bowls, none
  Championship seasons, none
  Colors: black, gold, white

San Francisco 49ers, 1946
  Super Bowl winner, 1982
  Other championship seasons, 1970 (division), 1971 (division), 1972 (division), 1983 (division)
  Colors: gold, scarlet

AMERICAN CONFERENCE

EASTERN DIVISION

Buffalo Bills, 1960
Super Bowls, none
Championship seasons, 1964 (AFL), 1965 (AFL), 1966 (division), 1980 (division)
Colors: scarlet, blue, white

Indianapolis Colts, 1953 (Baltimore Colts until 1984)
Super Bowl winner, 1971
Super Bowl runner-up, 1969
Other championship seasons, 1958 (NFL), 1959 (NFL), 1964 (conference), 1975 (division), 1976 (division), 1977 (division)
Colors: blue, white, silver

Miami Dolphins, 1966
Super Bowl winner, 1973, 1974
Super Bowl runner-up, 1972, 1983
Other championship seasons, 1974 (division), 1979 (division), 1981 (division), 1983 (division)
Colors: aqua, orange

New England Patriots, 1960 (Boston Patriots until 1971)
Super Bowls, none
Championship seasons, 1963 (division), 1978 (division)
Colors: red, blue, white

New York Jets, 1960 (New York Titans until 1963)
Super Bowl winner, 1969
Other championship season, 1969 (division)
Colors: green, white

CENTRAL DIVISION

Cincinnati Bengals, 1968
    Super Bowl runner-up, 1982
    Other championship seasons, 1970 (division), 1973
(division)
    Colors: orange, black, white

Cleveland Browns, 1946
    Super Bowls, none
    Championship seasons, 1946 (All-America Football
Conference), 1947 (AAFC), 1948 (AAFC), 1949 (AAFC), 1950
(NFL), 1951 (conference), 1952 (conference), 1953
(conference), 1954 (NFL), 1955 (NFL), 1964 (NFL), 1965
(conference), 1967 (division), 1968 (conference), 1969
(conference), 1971 (division), 1980 (division)
    Colors: brown, orange, white

Houston Oilers, 1960
    Super Bowls, none
    Championship seasons, 1960 (AFL), 1961 (AFL), 1962
(division), 1967 (division)
    Colors: scarlet, blue, white

Pittsburgh Steelers, 1933 (Pittsburgh Pirates until 1941)
    Super Bowl winner, 1975, 1976, 1979, 1980
    Other championship seasons, 1972 (division), 1973
(division), 1976 (division), 1977 (division), 1983 (division)
    Colors: black, gold

WESTERN DIVISION

Denver Broncos, 1960
   Super Bowl runner-up, 1978
   Other championship season, 1978 (division)
   Colors: orange, blue, white

Kansas City Chiefs, 1960 (founded as Dallas Texans, moved
to Kansas City, 1963)
   Super Bowl winner, 1970
   Super Bowl runner-up, 1967
   Other championship seasons, 1962 (AFL), 1971 (division)
   Colors: red, gold

Los Angeles Raiders, 1960 (founded as Oakland Raiders,
moved to Los Angeles, 1982)
   Super Bowl winner, 1977, 1981, 1984
   Super Bowl runner-up, 1968
   Other championship seasons, 1968 (division), 1969
(division), 1970 (division), 1972 (division), 1973 (division),
1974 (division), 1975 (division)
   Colors: silver, black

San Diego Chargers, 1960 (moved from Los Angeles, 1961)
   Super Bowls, none
 Championship seasons, 1960 (division), 1961 (division),
1963 (AFL), 1964 (division), 1965 (division), 1979 (division),
1980 (division), 1981 (division)
   Colors: blue, gold, white

Seattle Seahawks, 1976
   Super Bowls, none
   Championship seasons, none
   Colors: green, blue, silver

About the Author

Hal Lundgren is editor of *Texas Sportsworld*, a regional magazine that began publishing in 1984. He is a former pro football writer for the *Houston Cronicle* and public relations director for the San Francisco 49ers.

Mr. Lundgren has served as a member of the Pro Football Hall of Fame selections committee, president of Houston Sportswriters and Sportscasters Association, and Houston board of directors of Big Brothers-Big Sisters. He is married and has two sons. He enjoys playing the trumpet and the stock market, basketball, fishing, swimming, and classical music.

Mr. Lundgren has written other books for Childrens Press: *Earl Campbell: The Texas Tornado, Calvin Murphy: The Giant Slayer, Moses Malone: Philadelphia's Peerless Center,* and *Mary Lou Retton: Gold Medal Gymnast.*